Walking With Dead People
People
a self-guided tour

Mary-Beth Brophy

ISBN: 0-9893384-0-1
ISBN-13: 978-0-9893384-0-0

CONTENTS

INTRODUCTION

Welcome to Walking With Dead People - Hollywood. For the next hour and a half, I'll be taking you on a detour into the darker side of Hollywood. If you're interested in learning about the architecture of old buildings, or hearing happy stories about cute starlets getting discovered at soda fountain counters, boy have you come on the wrong tour. But, if you want to hear tales of mischief, murder and malevolent spirits, then I'm your gal.

Now, before we start, I do have to make a couple of disclaimers. This is a walking tour that will cover approximately two miles. I do not have a bus, pedal cart or 60-foot yacht hidden anywhere in this book. Nor will pressing any buttons on your phone produce comfortable shoes, a harem of litter bearers, or a stretch limo. If at any time, you are too tired or blister-ridden to continue on with the tour, you are responsible for locating your own rest stops. Oh for you out-of-towners, you could wait all day on a corner trying to hail a cab in Hollywood. There are two metro stations along our route – one at the corner of Hollywood Boulevard and Highland Avenue, and another at the corner of

Hollywood and Vine. There are also generally taxis at the Renaissance Hotel on Highland, just above the Hollywood and Highland Center

The tour will take us down Hollywood Boulevard to Vine and back again, with a couple of side trips. During that time, all traffic laws for the city of Los Angeles will remain in effect. Please stay on the sidewalk whenever possible and look both ways before crossing the street. I want you all to survive the tour so that you can tell your friends what a great time you had, so please be careful.

To begin the tour, make your way to the Roosevelt Hotel on Hollywood Boulevard (cross street is Orange Drive). Stand on Hollywood Boulevard facing Orange Drive with the hotel on your right hand side. The tour will take you east on Hollywood Boulevard to Vine Street with a few trips onto side streets. At Vine, you will cross the street and turn back toward the Roosevelt, finishing the tour just across the street at Grauman's Chinese Theatre. Directions to the next stop on the tour will appear at the end of every story.

ROOSEVELT HOTEL

Corner of Hollywood Boulevard and Orange Drive

Welcome to the Roosevelt Hotel, home to the first Academy Awards presentation in 1929.

The Roosevelt Hotel was built in 1927 and for many years it was *the* place to go star gazing. If you wandered out by the pool during Hollywood's golden years, you stood a reasonable chance is seeing Betty Grable, Ethel Merman or Gypsy Rose Lee. Marilyn Monroe posed for her very first ad on the diving board. Supernaturally speaking though, the hotel didn't become interesting until 1984, when it was closed for a two-year renovation. Some psychics believe that changing the physical structure of a building can awaking dormant spirits, and that certainly seems to be the case with the Roosevelt.

Employees helping to ready the hotel for its reopening complained of cold spots and inexplicable slamming doors. One woman started polishing a full length mirror in the general manager's office and found herself staring at the reflection of Marilyn Monroe. Two psychics later "read" the mirror and each sensed a feeling of great sadness. It turned out that the mirror had once hung in suite 1200, where Monroe was a regular guest.

The paranormal experiences continued after the hotel opened again to the public. The floors were reopened in stages, and hotel switchboard operators got regular late night calls from unoccupied rooms, including ones that had no phone. In 1989, an operator received several calls from room 1221, which was unoccupied. Each time, security was sent to the room, and they found that the guest phone had been taken off the hook. Other staff members complained of being pushed by unseen forces, seeing typewriters operate by themselves and having clipboards teleported into ice machines.

And then there are the actual apparitions. Several guests and employees have reporting seeing a man in a white tuxedo in and around the Blossom Room, where the original Academy Awards were presented. Each time, when the approached the man, he disappeared. At another time, a switchboard operator spotted a young girl in a ponytail and a pink jacket playing by the fountain in the lobby. Moments later, the girl vanished. And on another occasion, security cameras showed a man swimming in the hotel pool late at night. When a security guard arrived to tell the man that that swimming hours were over, he found the pool was empty – even though his coworker could still see the swimmer on camera.

But probably the most active ghost in the Roosevelt has to be Montgomery Clift, who stayed in room 928 for three months in 1952 while filming "From Here to Eternity." Apparently, Clift liked to roam the halls on the ninth floor, rehearsing his lines and playing his bugle. I'll bet his neighbors just loved that. He didn't learn courtesy in the afterlife either. Visitors to the ninth floor have reported being brushed against by an unseen force, and several staff members refused to work on the floor at all, claiming to have seen shadows and sensed something "strange" and disturbing. One guest in room 928 was reading in bed when someone patted her on the shoulder. She turned to her husband, only to find that he was fast asleep.

If all of this ghostly activity was caused by the hotel renovations, it's interesting to note that the Roosevelt just completed significant work in the lobby and is in the process of refurbishing all of the guest rooms. It'll be interesting to see if more of the hotel's permanent guests decide to make appearances this time around.

Cross Orange Drive, and walk east on Hollywood Boulevard, stopping at the El Capitan Theatre. Then, position yourself so that you can look across the Boulevard into the Hollywood and Highland Centre and see a second-floor cross bridge at the back of the main courtyard.

EL CAPITAN THEATRE

6838 Hollywood Boulevard

Stop at the view of the Hollywood Sign

If the weather is clear, you can get a great view of the Hollywood sign from that walkway. So head on up there before continuing with this section.

The sign was built in 1923 to advertise a housing development. It originally spelled out Hollywoodland and each letter was outlined in 20-watt light bulbs. In 1929, a young theater actress named Lillian Millicent Entwistle came to Hollywood to break into the movies. Lillian, or Peg, as she liked to be called, didn't have much luck with the studios and only landed a few parts over the next three years. And so, on September 18, 1932, she climbed a workman's ladder to the top of the "H" in the Hollywoodland sign and jumped to what she assumed would be her death. Unfortunately for Peg, she landed on a cactus rather than the hard ground, and suffered through several surgeries before dying in the hospital a few days later. Ironically, shortly after her leap of despair, Peg received a letter from the Beverly Hills Community Players offering her the lead in their next production. Her character was a woman who commits suicide.

The Hollywoodland housing development never lived up to its expectations and, in 1939, the developer stopped maintaining the sign, which soon fell into disrepair. In 1949, the "H" that Peg had thrown herself from fell over. Several efforts were made to restore the sign until finally, it 1978, a massive fundraising effort was launched and the sign was restored to its present condition. Like the sign, Peg Entwistle also remains a part of the local landscape. Hikers in the area have reported seeing her ghost walking towards the sign, still wearing the white dress she wore on that fateful day in 1932.

If you are on the cross bridge, return to El Capitan and stand with the theatre on your right. Walk east on Hollywood Boulevard until you come to Jean Harlow's star on the Walk of Fame. If you reach Highland Avenue, you have gone too far.

JEAN HARLOW'S WALK OF FAME STAR

6910 Hollywood Boulevard

In 1930, silver screen siren Jean Harlow, whose real name was Harlean Carpentier, became an overnight star in the Howard Hughes film, *Hells Angels.* The 19-year-old Harlow, who had already had one marriage annulled, quickly became known as much for her off-screen antics as she was for her movie roles in such films as *Bombshell, Dinner at Eight,* and *Public Enemy.* Women across the country tried to emulate her platinum blond look and her comment that "a brassiere is an unnecessary garment," actually sent underwear sales plummeting.

Sadly, although she was reportedly a millionaire by the age of 26, Harlow seemed to live under a dark cloud. Her second husband, MGM producer Paul Bern, shot himself while Harlow was away visiting her mother, leaving behind a note to her which read, "Dearest Dear, Unfortunately, this is the only way to make good the frightful wrong I have done you, and to wipe out my abject humiliation. I love you. Paul."

Over the next few years, Harlow married and divorced a third husband, and fell increasingly under the control of her mother "Mama Jean" and stepfather, who managed her career. In 1936, she was suspended by MGM after her stepfather tried to negotiate more money as part of her contract. All was soon forgiven though and in May of 1937, she was filming *Saratoga* with Clark Gable when she suddenly turned to her makeup artist with a strange premonition. According to newspaper reports, Harlow said, "You know, Violet, I have a hunch I'm going away from here and never coming back." She was right. Later that day, she collapsed on the set and was taken home.

She spent the next two weeks being nursed at home by her mother, a devout Christian Scientist. Depending on who you believe, Harlow either took a sudden turn for the worse after two weeks of home care, or she grew steadily sicker while her mother drove away those who came to see her until her former agent finally insisted that an ambulance be called. Either way, she died several hours after being admitted to the hospital for uremic poisoning. She was 26 years old.

Continue east on Hollywood Boulevard until you reach Highland Avenue. Stop before crossing the street.

MAX FACTOR BUILDING/HOLLYWOOD MUSEUM

1660 Highland Avenue

In 1928, the famous make-up artist Max Factor bought the property on the eastern side of the street and completely renovated it into the ornate pink building you see today. At the time, the section of Hollywood resembled Rodeo Drive, and the building served as a combination of laboratory, factory, cosmetics shop and beauty parlor, dedicated to making celebrities and society ladies look stunning.

Max Factor reigned as the King of Movie Make-up from the mid-1920s until his death in 1938, and the stories behind his entry into and exit from Hollywood were the stuff movies are made of. He began his career in Russia in the court of Tsar Nicholas the Second, where he was given the title of cosmetics expert to several members of the royal entourage, as well as the Imperial Russian Grand Opera. But life wasn't all wine and roses for Max. As a member of the court, he was forbidden to become romantically involved with anyone, and was only allowed to leave the palace once a week, under guard.

Max was a clever young man though and managed to make the most of his days off. In fact, he courted, married and fathered three children with a young woman named Esther Rose. Since the Tsar wasn't known for allowing his employees to simply resign, Max used his make-up kit to fake an illness and escaped his guard while on route to a resort where he was expected to recuperate. Together with his family, he boarded a boat for America and the Russian Royal family's loss became Hollywood's gain.

Unfortunately, the intrigues in Max's life didn't always have a happy ending. In 1938, while on his way to Rome, the 66-year-old makeup mogul became the victim of a rather strange extortion attempt. He received a note demanding that he deliver $200 to the Eiffel Tower. If he refused, the note promised that he would be killed. A stand-in made up to look like Max went to the rendezvous spot, but the extortionist did not show up to collect his $200. Max seemed to have taken the threat to heart though, because he returned home, took to his bed and soon died. Perhaps he should have delivered that $200 himself.

The building now houses the Hollywood Museum, which is

well worth a stop – or a return trip if you are pressed for time today. Max Factor's make-up rooms have been restore –featuring different colored décor to suit various hair and skin tones. The rest of the building houses an extensive costume and memorabilia collection, from the dog in There's Something About Mary to Hannibal Lector's prison cell.

The next stop on the tour can be viewed from where you are standing. Look diagonally across Hollywood Boulevard to your left. The building on the northeast corner is the Hollywood First National Bank.

HOLLYWOOD FIRST NATIONAL BANK

6777 Hollywood Boulevard

You may recognize the building on the northeastern side of the corner: the Hollywood First National Bank. It was built in 1927 and was, for one brief year, the tallest building in Los Angeles. Later, in the 1950's, actor George Reeves could be seen every week taking flight from the building's rooftop on *The Adventures of Superman.* In the summer of 1959, George Reeves allegedly took his own life in the midst of a noisy dinner party in his Benedict Canyon Home. But Reeves has not rested in peace, a fact which has given rise to theories that the man of steel was actually murdered. In the years that followed, Reeves appeared to a number of people in and around his former home, often in full Superman regalia. It seems he found a way to live on forever, if only through his character.

Cross Highland Avenue and walk approximately two blocks east on Hollywood Boulevard to the Egyptian Theatre.

EGYPTIAN THEATRE

6712 Hollywood Boulevard

We're standing in front of the Egyptian theatre, which was built by Sid Grauman in 1922. The theatre was originally intended to resemble a palace, but when King Tut's tomb was unearthed in 1921, Grauman ordered the original designs scrapped in favor of an Egyptian theme. Grauman was considered by many to be the ultimate Hollywood showman, and there is no doubt that he knew how to put on a spectacle. He unveiled his new theatre with what has been credited as the world's first movie premiere, complete with spotlights, tasseled ropes and a high ticket price for Douglas Fairbank's production, *Robin Hood*. Unfortunately, Grauman quickly lost interest in the Egyptian, moving down the street just five years later to open Grauman's Chinese Theatre, where we'll end the tour.

But that's all official history. So why are we stopping here, in front of the Egyptian? Well, Grauman's love of spectacle apparently extended into his personal life, and he was well known among his friend for his elaborate and often twisted practical jokes. He also liked to play with wax dummies and those two interests combined with rather startling results. According to Hollywood legend, he once invited the original owner of Loews Theaters, Marcus Loew to his suite at the Ambassador Hotel on Wilshire Boulevard and told him that he had 75 movie theater owners waiting in the darkened room to hear about upcoming MGM movies. Loew gave an impromptu speech to the gathering before he realized that they were actually waxworks.

One of Grauman's more perverse pranks involved Charlie Chaplin. Again, from his suite in the Ambassador Hotel, Grauman called Chaplin and begged him to come over. On arrival, Chaplin found Grauman huddled over what appeared to be murdered woman in his bed, covered in blood. Grauman claimed to have no idea how the dead woman got there and begged Chaplin to help him cover it up. Only after Chaplin repeatedly insisted that Grauman call the police, did he reveal that the dead woman was really a wax dummy drenched in ketchup.

Given the questionable taste of Grauman's jokes, it's understandable that many of the victims did not want to talk about the details of their ordeals. His 1950 obituary acknowledged that he was a "great gagger" and left it at that.

Continue east on Hollywood Boulevard to Thomas Edison's Walk of Fame Star at the corner of Hollywood Boulevard and Las Palmas Avenue.

THOMAS EDISON'S WALK OF FAME STAR

6700 Hollywood Boulevard

Thomas Edison isn't exactly a name that most people expect to see on the Walk of Fame. Edison's company owned the patent for motion picture cameras made in America, or more specifically, for the number of sprocket holes used in the film. He established the Edison Trust to police the motion picture industry and ensure that filmmakers didn't get around paying licensing fees by purchasing their cameras from Europe, where Edison had unfortunately neglected to patent his invention in time. Early movie moguls came to Los Angeles as much to evade the Edison Trust as to take advantage of the warm weather.

Trust agents were dedicated though and they often traveled to Los Angeles to spy on films that were in production here. If they found a film being made with unlicensed equipment, they weren't opposed to shooting out the lenses in the camera in order to halt production. And they didn't lose too much sleep if they hit the odd camera man with a stray bullet or two. Cecil B. DeMille, director of the first feature length film, was rumored to be so frightened of the Edison Trust that he guarded his finished film, the Squaw Man at gunpoint in the days before its release.

Turn left onto Las Palmas Avenue, and walk south for one block to Selma Avenue. Cross Selma, veer right, and continue down Las Palmas Avenue for one more block to Sunset Boulevard. Turn left, and stop at the entrance to Crossroads of the World.

CROSSROADS OF THE WORLD

6671 Sunset Boulevard

If you've seen the movie "L.A. Confidential," you might just recognize the office block behind this fence as the headquarters of the newspaper tabloid, the Tattler. Crossroads of the World opened in 1936 as the first shopping mall in Los Angeles and, if you walk around to its main entrance on Sunset Boulevard, you'll see that it was built to resemble a cruise ship. But I didn't bring you all the way down here for the architecture. Just five years before Crossroads of the World opened, this spot housed the real estate offices of Charlie Crawford, a local underworld figure and owner of the weekly magazine, "The Critic of Critics." In 1931, Crawford was found shot to death in his office along with the Critic's editor, Herbert Spencer.

Twenty-four hours later, David Clark, a war hero, former deputy district attorney and current candidate for municipal court judge, confessed to committing the crime. Despite his indictment for double-murder, Clark persisted with his candidacy for judgeship and garnered 60,000 votes, although he ultimately lost the election. "Handsome Dave," as he came to be known, claimed he had shot the two men in self-defense, although no weapons were recovered from Crawford's office. Nonetheless, he secured a hung jury in his first trial and was acquitted by a second jury just five months after the murder.

Clark didn't elude justice forever though. In 1954, he pled guilty to second degree murder after shooting his former law partner's wife. It's a little unclear how Mrs. Crawford felt about the untimely death of her husband. She had the building where he had been murdered torn down and commissioned Crossroads of the World to be built on the spot. I suppose we'll never know why she thought that a fake cruise ship shopping mall was a fitting tribute to his memory.

Retrace your steps to the corner of Las Palmas and Selma Avenues. Stand with the back of Crossroads of the World on your right, and continue east on Selma for a block. Turn left onto North Cherokee Avenue, and walk back toward Hollywood Boulevard on the right side of the street, stopping at Boardner's.

BOARDNER'S

1652 North Cherokee Avenue

Steve Boardner's bar has been serving some of the best margaritas in Los Angeles since the 1930s. In the mid-1940s, Boardner's was a popular hangout for many of the hundreds of young women who came to Hollywood hoping to become a movie star and marrying a war hero. In reality, many of the girls lived on the brink of homelessness, often sharing a single room with four or five other girls. The lucky ones found jobs as junior hostesses, dancing with servicemen at the Hollywood Canteen or the USO Club. The rest depended, in the words of Scarlett O'Hara, on the kindness of strangers, for meals and money.

One of those women was a striking brunette named Elizabeth Short. In September of 1946, she was living with several other women in an apartment just north of here, at 1842 North Cherokee. She was a recognizable character on the local scene, wearing dramatic makeup that made her look almost like a geisha. Some soldier in Long Beach even gave her the nickname, the Black Dahlia, after a Veronica Lake movie that was playing at the time. But her friends knew another, more private side—a girl who used wax to fill the cavities in her rotting teeth and wrote letters to servicemen about love affairs that seemed to exist only in her mind.

Poor Elizabeth never became a movie star or a serviceman's wife. She was last seen alive on the night of January 9, 1947, in the lobby of the Biltmore hotel downtown. She was dropped off by a man she had met in San Diego and hung around for a while, apparently waiting for somebody. Then, she walked out the front entrance, and disappeared into the arms of a killer.

Her body was found six days later in a vacant lot about seven miles from the hotel. She had been stabbed and her skin was peeled away in places. The corners of her mouth had been cut, widening her smile almost to her ears. Some of her internal organs were missing, and she had been chopped in half at the waist. The killer then gave Elizabeth a bath, and washed and styled her hair. Finally, he left her body posed by the side of the road.

In life, Elizabeth Short was just a girl from Medford, Massachusetts. In death, she became the Black Dahlia, Hollywood's most famous unsolved murder victim. More than forty people confessed to committing the crime, and the police arrested, interrogated and released two official suspects. But the real killer was never caught. Officially, the case is still open and the file is assigned to an LAPD homicide detective. Unofficially, the police have long since stopped searching for the person or persons who brutally ended Elizabeth Short's life on that winter day more than fifty years ago.

Of course, not everyone lost interest in the case. There have been a lot of theories over the years. Some said it was the traveling salesman who dropped her off at the Biltmore. Others thought it was a tall soldier with a limp, the same anonymous man who allegedly murdered a wealthy Hollywood socialite in her bathtub a few years earlier. One woman even blamed the Dahlia's death on Orson Welles, and claimed he left clues about the murder in his movie "The Lady from Shanghai." And recently, a retired police detective became the second person to write a book claiming to be the son or daughter of the Black Dahlia's killer.

One of the more credible theories deals with a nightclub owner named Mark Hanson. Several months before she died, Elizabeth began hanging out at Hanson's club, the Florentine Gardens, and moved into a house he owned. Hanson was purported to be involved with Elizabeth's friend and had allegedly promised Elizabeth a part in one of the club's upcoming floor shows.

But in December of 1946, Elizabeth suddenly fled to San Diego. She told several people that someone had attacked her, and she had deep scratches on her arms to prove it. One night, two men and a woman came looking for her at the house where she was staying, and Elizabeth hid until they went away. The next day, she returned to Los Angeles and promptly disappeared.

After her death, some of her belongings were soaked in gasoline and then anonymously sent to a local newspaper. One of the items was an address book she had apparently stolen from Mark Hanson, with several pages removed. While the police questioned Hanson, they never investigated him seriously as a suspect. But if you believe that Elizabeth Short knew her killer, then he stands out as an interesting suspect. Of course, it's just a theory, and there have been plenty of them over the years. The reality is, we'll probably never know who killed the Black Dahlia.

While Boardner's was renovated a number of years ago and has lost a bit of its dive bar allure, it's still well worth a stop to wet your whistle.

Continue north on Cherokee Avenue. Turn right onto Hollywood Boulevard, and stop at Arthur Lake's Walk of Fame Star.

ARTHUR LAKE'S WALK OF FAME STAR

6646 Hollywood Boulevard

Arthur Lake is best known for playing Dagwood Bumstead in the Blondie movies in the 1940s and during a short-lived tv series in the 1950s. But it was his personal life, not his film career, that earned him a spot on this tour. You see, Arthur was married to a young woman Patricia van Cleve, a favorite niece of character actress Marion Davies. Davies was the longtime mistress of newspaper magnate William Randolph Hearst. We'll talk a little more about their relationship later on in the tour, but for now we'll focus on their heirs.

Officially, Hearst and Davies had no children together. However, the couple were very close to Davies' niece, Patricia van Cleve. They were present at her marriage to actor Arthur Lake and Davies even gave the couple a lavish estate in Bel Air. And when Lake and van Cleve died, they were interred inside Davies crypt at

Hollywood Forever Cemetery on Melrose Avenue. Shortly after van Cleve's death, her family revealed that she was indeed the daughter of both Hearst and Davies. However, that claim has never been substantiated.

In addition to having possibly married William Randolph Hearst's love child, Arthur Lake has a brief, but very odd connection to the Black Dahlia murder. Apparently, Lake frequented the Hollywood USO Canteen on Cahuenga Boulevard during World War 2. The Canteen was a favorite hangout for both the Black Dahlia, Elizabeth Short, and another young woman she knew, socialite Georgette Bauerdorf. Georgette was found brutally murdered in her bathtub several years before Elizabeth Short died and many Black Dahlia sleuths believe that the two murders were the work of one man.

When the girls were both still alive, Elizabeth Short had a conversation with Arthur Lake at the Canteen, and he told her that she looked just like Georgette. In retrospect, it was prophetic comparison for Lake to have made, and it lends credibility to the idea that they might have been attacked by the same man, particularly since neither killer was ever caught.

Walk east on Hollywood Boulevard one long block to Schrader Boulevard. Look across Hollywood Boulevard for a pink and white building called the Hudson Apartments.

HILLVIEW APARTMENTS

6541 Hollywood Boulevard

Okay, stay with me on this. The building housing the Hudson Apartments across the street is a replica of the original Hillview Apartments, which stood on the same location before being damaged first by the 1994 Northridge earthquake and later by a fire. The pinkish building you see today isn't the Hillview Apartments but a fairly accurate copy. So you are basically looking at what you would have seen if you were standing on this same corner about 90 years ago. Are you following that? Good because explaining it twice always gives me a headache.

Today, most people would be thrilled to have a celebrity leaving next door, but that hasn't always been the case. Hollywood was originally founded by Horace and Daeida Wilcox 1887 as a temperance community. They forbade saloons on their land and offered free land to anyone who wanted to build a church.

Needless to say, the film industry didn't measure up to their high moral standards. In fact, in the early nineteen hundreds, it was quite common for boarding houses in Hollywood to display a sign in the window which read, "No actors, no dogs." And I think they were willing to be a bit more flexible with the dogs.

But you can't stop progress and early movie mogul Jesse Lasky, whose Lasky's Feature Play Company later merged with Zukor's Famous Players and eventually became Paramount Studios, came up with a very practical solution to the problem. He built his own apartments, specifically for silent film actors. Hillview Apartments went up in 1917, but as of a few years ago they had fallen into disrepair. As you can see, the building has been recently restored as upscale apartments, maintaining the same layout and general architecture of the original building. Ironically, these apartments are well out of the price range of most working actors today.

If you crossed Hollywood Boulevard for a closer look at the Hillview/Hudson Apartments, retrace your steps so that you are once again on the right side of the street. Cross Schrader Boulevard, and continue east on Hollywood Boulevard to Alfred Hitchcock's Walk of Fame Star. If you reach Wilcox Avenue, you have gone too far.

ALFRED HITCHCOCK'S WALK OF FAME STAR

6506 Hollywood Boulevard

Alfred Hitchcock achieved legendary status for his innovative and often disturbing movies. Even so, he wasn't the most popular person with actors and movie censors, owing to his rather unorthodox style, both on and off screen. I'm sure you are all familiar with the movie ratings used today – G, PG, PG-13, R and M-17. Back in the thirties, forties and fifties though, movies were governed by strict standards, and if you broke one of many standards set by the movie censors, your film simply could not be released in the United States.

As a director, Hitchcock knew these standards well and he occasionally like to play with them. For example, when his movie *Notorious* was released in 1946, an onscreen kiss could be no more than three seconds in duration. Well, if you've seen the movie, you know that stars Ingrid Bergman and Cary Grant shared a very long, passionate kiss.

Hitchcock got around the codes by having them kiss for three seconds, talk a little, kiss some more, break apart, kiss some more, and so on. The movie audience got to see a lot more action than they were used to, and the movie censors could do nothing to stop it. Later, in 1960, Hitchcock broke another longstanding, if unofficial, movie taboo, when his movie *Psycho* became the first film released in America to show a toilet being flushed.

Hitchcock liked to play with his actors as well. During the filming of *The Thirty-Nine Steps*, he handcuffed co-stars Madeleine Carroll and Robert Donat together for a scene, and then claimed to have lost the key to the cuffs for several hours. According to some sources, the director was waiting to see how his interconnected stars would handle the inevitable calls of nature.

While filming *Psycho*, Hitchcock used Vivian Leigh to experiment with effects that would make his audience scream. As he developed versions of Norman Bates' mother's corpse, he would leave the dummies for Vivian to find unexpectedly. Once he found a dummy that truly terrified her, he used it in the film.

The next stop on the tour is the corner of Hollywood and Vine. Walk east on Hollywood Boulevard for approximately four blocks. There is nothing physical to see at Hollywood and Vine anymore (just some interesting stories to tell) so, if you would like to shave two blocks off your walk, stop at Ivar Avenue instead.

If you are too tired to finish the tour, you can also continue on to Hollywood and Vine, where there is a Metro stop. If you take the Red Line toward North Hollywood, you can get off at the Hollywood and Highland stop, which is very near the start of the tour. Then you can return to the Hollywood and Vine Metro stop to continue your tour on another day.

HOLLYWOOD AND VINE

Corner of Hollywood Boulevard and Vine Street

If you talk to Hollywood locals, many will tell you rather snootily that absolutely nothing ever happened at Los Angeles' most famous intersection. Well that's not necessarily true, at least from a supernatural perspective. In fact, two of movieland's biggest horror movie actors left their marks on Hollywood and Vine—Lon Chaney and Bela Lugosi.

Lon Chaney, star of such movie classics as the *Phantom of the Opera* and the *Hunchback of Notre Dame*, was apparently a fan of public transportation and would catch the bus almost daily at the corner of Hollywood and Vine. For many years after his death in 1930, Chaney's sharply dressed ghost was frequently seen sitting on his regular bench, awaiting the next bus to the studios. Finally, the bench was removed and Chaney's ghost move on. Or perhaps he simply caught his bus at last.

Phantom of the Opera was filmed at Universal Studios' sound stage 28 which is still used for productions. Studio employees and visitors to the historic stage have reported seeing a man in a dark cape running along the catwalks above the stage. Many believe that the ghost, who apparently enjoys meddling with doors and lights, is none other than the phantom of the opera himself, Lon Chaney.

After Chaney's death, studio executives had to hurriedly recast his next project, *Dracula*. Fortunately, they found the perfect replacement in the relatively unknown Hungarian actor Bela Lugosi. Although Lugosi was immortalized by his turn as *Dracula*, he eventually became addicted to heroin and finished his life and his career in a series of strange movies for the king of bad movies, Ed Wood.

Wood was such a believer in the sentiment, 'the show must go on,' that he continued filming *Plan 9 from Outer Space* even after his star had succumbed to his drug addiction, using a stunt double and shooting Lugosi's scenes from behind. He finished the picture and started a rather dubious tradition that has been continued in such movies as *Poltergeist 3* and *Queen of the Damned*.

During his lifetime, Lugosi loved walking up and down Hollywood Boulevard. However, at the time of his death in 1953, store owners on the boulevard objected to the possibility that funeral processions might dampen the moods of their patrons, so funeral director obliged and avoided the street. However, when the hearse carrying Bela Lugosi's body reached Hollywood Boulevard, it apparently turned of its own accord and paraded down the street for one block before continuing it's scheduled journey. The vehicle's driver claimed that an unseen force took control of the wheel for the short ride.

The corner of Hollywood and Vine is the midpoint of the tour. To continue, cross to the north side of Hollywood Boulevard, and begin walking back in the direction of the Roosevelt Hotel. To get to the next stop, turn right at Ivar Avenue. If you skipped the last block and are standing on the right side of Hollywood Avenue at Ivar, turn left onto Ivar, walking north on the right side of the street.

KNICKERBOCKER HOTEL

1714 North Ivar Avenue

The Knickerbocker Hotel was built in 1925. Today, the building is a retirement home. However, over the years the Knickerbocker has been the scene of some rather bizarre goings-on, starting in the 1920s when Rudolph Valentino was rumored to ride his horse to the hotel when he wanted a drink.

Escape artist Harry Houdini spent the latter part of his life attempting to discredit the mediums and psychic channelers who had cropped up across America and Europe, taking money from grieving widows and parents in exchange for a chance to contact loved ones on the other side. But in the years before he died he started to wonder if in fact it was possible to make contact with deceased loved ones.

He and his wife Bess promised each other that the first to die would attempt to contact the other from beyond the grave, using a secret code they had devised. Harry, of course, died first. According to rumor, he lost his life as a result of injuries from a poorly timed punch by a fan he had invited to punch him as hard as possible, in order to test the strength of his abdominal muscles.

For ten years after Houdini's death, Bess held regular séances in an attempt to contact her husband. And on Halloween night in 1936, she attended her tenth and final séance on the roof of the Knickerbocker. Although she originally signed an affidavit revealing that Harry did use their code to contact her that night, Bess later retracted her statement. So we'll never really know whether the greatest escape artist of all time was able to pull off the ultimate escape, and pierce the veil between this world and the next.

In 1943, actress Frances Farmer was dragged naked, wrapped only in a shower curtain, through the lobby of the hotel to a waiting police car, screaming obscenities at her captors. The volatile Farmer had been arrested for drunk driving, and then violated the conditions of her probation by skipping regular appointments with her parole officer.

Frances was not known for holding her tongue—in fact, she was often heard to say that she hated everything about Hollywood except the money. During her court hearing, she threw an ink pot at the judge and later assaulted a police matron and another cop. She paid dearly for her actions when she was imprisoned and subsequently institutionalized. Eventually, Farmer underwent a lobotomy and the world lost a gifted, if erratic, actress. All this, over a traffic stop.

In 1948, the Knickerbocker once again took center stage when film director D.W. Griffith, one of the founding fathers of modern day movie making, died of a cerebral hemorrhage in the hotel. According to one story, he actually dropped dead right in the lobby under the grand chandelier. But it's more likely that he actually died in his room at the Knickerbocker, penniless and nearly forgotten.

You'd think that after the misfortunes that befell Farmer and Griffith at the Knickerbocker, celebrities would avoid the Knickerbocker at all costs, but that just wasn't the case. In fact, Marilyn Monroe and Joe DiMaggio rendezvoused here quite regularly in the mid-1950s. But it wasn't until 1962 that the Knickerbocker would make its final sad stamp on Hollywood lore. Motion picture dress designer Irene Gibbons jumped to her death from the top floor of the hotel. Unfortunately, Irene failed to think her dramatic exit through. She landed, not on the ground, but on the lobby awning. As a result, her body wasn't discovered for several days, when guests began complaining about a strange smell.

Return to Hollywood Boulevard, turn right, and walk several blocks, stopping midway between Cahuenga Boulevard and Wilcox Avenue.

PACIFIC THEATRE

6423 Hollywood Boulevard

The Pacific Theater here on the corner is alleged to be haunted by the ghost of Sam Warner, one of the four Warner brothers. In the mid-1920s, the Warner brothers risked everything they had to make the *Jazz Singer*, the first "talkie" motion picture. The hoped to have this Warner Brothers' Theater finished in time for the movie's premiere, but it was not to be. When it became clear that the film would have to debut elsewhere, Sam Warner stood in the lobby of his unfinished theater and cursed it. Perhaps he should have been more careful with his words.

Twenty-four hours before the *Jazz Singer* debuted in New York, Sam Warner died of a brain hemorrhage in Los Angeles, where he had been overseeing the final work of the theater. In the decades since he died, Sam's ghost has been seen in the theater lobby, as well as in the administrative offices above. Apparently, Sam particularly likes to ride the elevator, which moves from floor to floor without being summoned.

Walk to the corner of Wilcox Avenue and look north across the street.

SUICIDE HOTEL

1735 North Wilcox Avenue

While the building is long gone, the stories connected to this address still earn themselves a stop on the tour. This was once the site of the Shelton Apartments, otherwise known as the Suicide Hotel. In the early 1900s, identical twins Jenny and Rosie Dolly gained fame as a vaudeville dance team. Throughout America and Europe, Jenny Dolly was as well known for her personal exploits as she was for her dancing abilities. She was an avid gambler and is rumored to have been the only woman to ever break the bank in Monte Carlo. If she was, she apparently didn't hold onto the money for long.

Those who knew her said that Jenny believed she was living under a dark cloud, in spite of her seeming success. In 1933, her predictions of doom seemed to come true when Jenny was hideously disfigured in a car accident, ending her once brilliant career. Eight years later, the ruined dancer ended her life in the Shelton apartments. She kept her flair for drama until the very end, hanging herself from a curtain rod in front of a window overlooking the Hollywood Hills.

One celebrity suicide might seem sufficient for any other location, but the Shelton Apartments had another part to play in Hollywood legend. Twenty-one years after Jenny Dolly's dramatic exit, Clara Blandick, best known as Dorothy's Auntie Em in the *Wizard of Oz*, also shrugged off her mortal coil at the Shelton. Ever the lady, Clara styled her hair, carefully applied her makeup and wrapped herself in a gold blanket before lying down on her coach and pulling a plastic bag over her head. Apparently, there really was no place like home at the Shelton.

The building was finally torn down in 1987, preventing future Hollywood unfortunates from following in Jenny and Dolly's footsteps.

Turn onto Wilcox Avenue and walk north to Yucca Street. Turn left onto Yucca, staying on the south side of the street.

LIDO APARTMENTS

6500 Yucca Street

Built in 1928, the Lido is the ultimate anti-success story. For many years, it was a swanky Venetian-style resort and the first address for many Broadway actors relocating from New York. Then it began a rather epic slide into ruin, culminating in the 1970s when the building's lobby was incorporating into the album art for the Eagles' *Hotel California*.

In 1979, actor Victor Kilian, who played the Fernwood Flasher on *Mary Hartman, Mary Hartman*, was murdered in his apartment here at the Lido, just days after turning 88. Known for playing rough and tumble characters – he lost an eye in a fight scene with John Wayne and is one of the relatively few actors who was able to resurrect a career after being blacklisted by the McCarthy panel - Kilian is thought to have struck up a conversation with a stranger at a local bar and invited the man back to his home. Kilian's body was found the next day in his burglarized apartment. His killer was never found.

In a bit of apparently grim coincidence, Kilian died just days after another actor, Charles Wagenheim, was also beaten to death during a burglary a few blocks away. While Wagenheim's killer was not a suspect in Kilian's death, both men had recently worked together on an episode of *All in the Family,* which aired after their deaths.

Curiously, Kilian's ghost has been seen repeatedly pacing the imprinted cement squares in the courtyard in front of Grauman's Chinese Theatre, where we'll end our tour. Since the Chinese Theatre doesn't fall between the Lido or the bar where Kilian met his killer,. perhaps his ghost is offering us a clue to his murderer's identity. Or maybe in death, Kilian has simply become the ultimate tourist, gaping at the handprints along with the rest of us.

Retrace your steps to Hollywood Boulevard, turn right, and continue walking west, stopping midway between Cherokee Avenue and Las Palmas Avenue.

JOHN BARRYMORE'S WALK OF FAME STAR

6667 Hollywood Boulevard

Hollywood is full of family dynasties and the Barrymores are probably the most famous. In the 1920s and 30s, siblings John, Ethel and Lionel Barrymore all made names for themselves on the stage and screen, appearing in such films as "Rasputin" and "Grand Hotel." John, the youngest of the three, was the first to die at the age of sixty on May 29, 1942. His death came as a terrible shock… to absolutely no one. Barrymore was a longtime alcoholic and his personal physician noted his "chronic carelessness in getting proper rest or observing even a semblance of diet."

John Barrymore was known for his wit and his turbulent affairs. Married and divorced four times, Barrymore downplayed his way with women, once saying, "No woman ever fell at my feet unless she was drunk or fainting." However, he didn't earn a spot on this tour by virtue of something he said or did, but rather something that was done with him.

According to Hollywood legend, John Barrymore became the central figure in a practical joke played on the notorious prankster Errol Flynn—the day *after* he died. Supposedly, some mutual friends of the two men convinced a funeral home director to let them borrow Barrymore's body for a private viewing. Instead, they took Barrymore to Flynn's house and propped him up in a chair. Depending on who's telling the story, Flynn either screamed upon his return home or offered the jokers a drink. In any case, Barrymore was apparently returned to the funeral home and buried without any further disruptions.

Cross Las Palmas Avenue. The next two stops on the tour are next to each other at the corner of Hollywood Boulevard and Las Palmas Avenue.

MARY ASTOR'S WALK OF FAME STAR

6701 Hollywood Boulevard

Mary Astor was a popular character actress in the 1930s and '40s. Her most famous role was likely her turn as the villainous Bridget O'Shaughnessy in The Maltese Falcon with Humphrey Bogart. However, her most juicy work didn't take place on the stage or screen, but rather in the pages of her diary. A one-time mistress of John Barrymore, Mary was an avid journal writer and she kept rather explicit accounts of her sexual exploits throughout the years.

Unfortunately for Mary, she did little to guard her secret scribblings and her physician husband, Dr. Franklyn Thorpe discovered Mary's 1935 edition, a volume which detailed her affair with playwright George S. Kaufman.

Thorpe retaliated by embarking on a series of affairs with

available starlets before taking custody of the diary and filing for divorce. The diary became part of the court record during the custody battle for their daughter Marilyn. Its contents were so steamy that although Mary won custody of her daughter, the court refused to return the diary, calling it pornography and ordering it burned.

Fortunately for Mary, the depression had gone a long way towards softening the public's view of celebrity indiscretions and her sordid divorce did little to damage her career. Our next star did not fare nearly as well.

ROSCOE ARBUCKLE'S WALK OF FAME STAR

6701 Hollywood Boulevard

Comic actor Roscoe "Fatty" Arbuckle enjoyed eight years of fame before scandal cut his career short in 1921. The 260 pound Hollywood heavyweight was discovered by movie producer Mack Sennett while working as a plumber's assistant. After starting out as a Keystone Cop for $3 a day, Arbuckle appeared in a series of slapstick comedies with the likes of Charlie Chaplin and Buster Keaton, and was headlining for Paramount Studios at a salary of $5,000 per week by 1917. Arbuckle's career nearly ended at the party he threw in Boston to celebrate his new contract with Paramount.

Police raided the party and discovered the twelve scantily clad young ladies who had been hired to "entertain" at the event.

Fortunately for Arbuckle, movie moguls Adolph Zukor, Jesse Lasky and Joseph Schenk were also in attendance. According to rumor, the three men paid $100,000 to prevent charges from being filed. Arbuckle should have quite while he was ahead, but he didn't.

In 1921, he threw another party, this one to celebrate a new three-million-dollar contract with Paramount. During the two-day celebration at the Hotel St. Francis in San Francisco, Arbuckle escorted actress and party girl Virginia Rappe, whom he had recently cast in one of his comedies, into suite 1221. What happened next was a subject of hot debate.

Some believe that Arbuckle raped Virginia, while others claim that Virginia's excessive drinking was the real culprit. In any case, Virginia was somehow injured in suite 1221 and rushed to a local hospital. She died several days later of peritonitis, apparently caused by a ruptured bladder. Arbuckle was charged with first-degree murder.

Unfortunately, the odds were not in Virginia's favor. Her party-girl lifestyle and the fact that any witnesses to the events surrounding the crime were drunken partygoers made justice elusive. After two hung juries, Arbuckle was eventually acquitted by a jury that was so star-struck it actually apologized to Arbuckle for his ordeal. But the incident was too shocking for Hollywood executives. Arbuckle's three-million-dollar contract was cancelled and he had to change his name to William Goodrich in order to gain sporadic employment as a comedy director. He died, nearly broke, in New York in 1933.

THE LOST HOLLYWOOD CAMEL
CARAVAN

Corner of Hollywood Boulevard and North Las Palmas Avenue

While nothing of note happened at this particular intersection, it's as good a place as any to share one of the more bizarre stories I've unearthed during my research into the area: the lost Hollywood Camel Caravan.

The film industry was founded by entrepreneurs – nobody knew anything about making movies, so it was anybody's business. Of course, not every new business proposition ends in resounding success. In fact, some of the ideas that have drawn people to Southern California could be considered doomed to failure. One such idea was the brainchild of settler George Caralambo, who came to the area in the mid-1800s.

Back then, Hollywood was nothing but farmland. George decided to set up a caravan route between the army posts that were scattered throughout California and New Mexico. Because the climate was so arid, he imported a herd of Turkish camels to carry supplies from post to post. The idea never really caught on though and camels were turned loose in what later became Hollywood.

Don't go looking for them behind Musso and Franks though; by the turn of the century, they had all disappeared. We can only speculate about what became of them.

To get to the next stop on the tour, turn right onto North McCadden Place and walk one block until the road ends at Yucca Street.

VILLA CAPRI

6735 Yucca Street

Unfortunately, the building that housed the Villa Capri restaurant was torn down in 1995 after local regulators determined that it had no architectural significance. Well, that may be, but... From 1950 through the early 1980s, this address was the site of the Villa Capri restaurant and bar, a favorite hangout of Rat Packers Frank Sinatra (who was a co-owner) and Sammy Davis Junior, as well Judy Garland, Humphrey Bogart and Lauren Bacall. But that's not even the most interesting thing about the restaurant, at least not on this tour. You see, this is where actor James Dean had his last supper.

On September 29, 1955, Dean stopped at the Villa Capri for dinner. As was his custom, he entered through the kitchen to avoid public notice. His recently purchased, silver Porche Spyder, which he had nicknamed "Little Bastard," sat in the parking lot while

Dean ate. The next day, he set off on a drive up the coast in "Little Bastard" with his friend and mechanic Rolf Wuetherich.

At the junction of Highway 41 and Route 466, "Little Bastard" collided with a car driven by a college student named, I kid you not, Donald Gene Turnupseed. Dean was killed instantly.

Now, there isn't any record that James Dean's spirit has lingered behind to haunt the Villa Capri or anywhere else. Still, the story is interesting for another reason. You see, there are many people who believe that "Little Bastard" was cursed.

Dean apparently told friends that he believed he was destined to die in a car accident. If that's the case, then he certainly got what he was looking for in "Little Bastard." The car had the power to make people uncomfortable. Actor Alec Guinness, displaying a rare bit of Obi Won Kenobi-like vision, advised Dean to get rid of the car immediately, and several other friends claimed that the car made them uncomfortable. But Dean wasn't to be dissuaded. And so, he died at 85 miles per hour behind the wheel of his Porche Spyder.

But the car wasn't finished. Following the accident, two prominent doctors purchased parts from the demolished Spyder for their racing cars. Both men inexplicably lost control of their cars during the same race; one was killed instantly and the other was badly injured. Later, two thieves were injured trying to steal parts from the demolished car as souvenirs. And after another man complained that the two tires he purchased from the wreckage had both exploded simultaneously,

"Little Bastard's" owner decided that things had gone far enough and put the car into storage. But the Porsche wouldn't rest quietly. When the owner agreed to allow the California Highway Patrol to display the junked vehicle as a lesson about the importance of safe driving, the destruction began again. During the safety tour, a garage where the car was being stored burned to the ground. At the very next stop, the car fell from a platform and badly injured a teenaged boy who was standing nearby. On route to Salinas, the city Dean had been heading for on his fatal trip, the truck carrying "Little Bastard" crashed. The car broke free and landed on the truck driver who had been thrown from the truck, killing him instantly.

Later, during "Little Bastard's" final public showing, the car inexplicably split into eleven pieces. Then, en route to a safety show in Florida, it simply disappeared and was never been seen again. One can't help but feel sorry anyone who has come in contact with its remains since.

Continue west on Yucca Street to the corner of Highland Avenue.

VIEW OF YAMASHIRO RESTAURANT

Corner of Yucca Street and Highland Avenue

If you look up the hill there, you'll see Yamashiro's restaurant. Yamashiro was built in 1914 by millionaire Adolph Bernheimer as an exact replica of a palace near Kyoto, Japan. At one time, it was home to "The 400 Club," a group made up of silent film celebrities like Lilian Gish and Ramon Novarro. According to rumor, the building served as a brothel during the depression when young actresses who couldn't find work on the silver screen made themselves available for other forms of entertainment. Shortly after the attack on Pearl Harbor, the house was vandalized by a mob who wrongly believed that it was a signal tower for Japanese attack planes. It was restored in 1948 and reopened as the Yamashiro restaurant.

If you'd like to see the restaurant up close, turn right onto Highland Avenue, walk a block, and turn left onto Franklin Avenue. Walk for about four blocks, and turn right again onto North Sycamore Avenue. When the road forks, bear left onto Fitch Drive, and then make a sharp right into the Yamashiro driveway. Then return walk back the way you came to Franklin for the next stop on the tour.

MAGIC CASTLE

7001 Franklin Avenue

The Magic Castle is a private club for magicians and magic enthusiasts. It was built in 1907 as a private home, but was taken over by Milt Larson and converted into the headquarters of the Academy of Magical Arts. If you've started to contemplate asking for a refund because you're midway through the tour and haven't seen any ghosts yet, then the Magic Castle may be just what you're looking for. Irma, the club's resident piano-playing wraith is on duty most nights. She has a wide repertoire and event takes requests. She is also quite happy to take tips, which can be dropped in the cage of her phantom pet bird.

If you have an opportunity to visit the Magic Castle, take it! Even the most resolute humbug is bound to find something to amuse. Entry through a hidden door requires a magic incantation, including magic shows, a staggering number of bars, and some interesting features, including a room paneled entirely with doors, WC Fields' pool table, a tabletop decorated with old Houdini keys, and a bar taken from the set of Hello Dolly.

The Castle enforces a strictly formal eveningwear dress code. Gentlemen –show up without a jacket and tie (and no, they don't mean a leather biker jacket) and you may be turned away or – perhaps worse – required to wear an embarrassingly styled loner for the evening. Ladies – rest assured that it's practically impossible to show up overdressed, so take the opportunity to wear that fabulous evening gown that never gets enough use.

There are several ways of getting into the Magic Castle. The first, and probably most difficult, is to audition for a magician membership. Other options include purchasing an associate membership, visiting with a member, obtaining a guest pass from a member, and taking a magic class (which includes access to the Castle during enrollment).

Once inside, don't restrict yourself to the Main Stage performances. There are shows in several smaller venues throughout the building, and magician members can often be found giving short performances in various nooks and crannies. It's well worth the trip!

Walk back to Highland Avenue and turn right Stop at the Hollywood and Highland Shopping Center.

HOTEL HOLLYWOOD

6801 Hollywood Boulevard

In 2001, the Hollywood and Highland shopping center opened as part of an effort to revitalize Hollywood. For reasons that are not entirely clear, it was modeled after D.W. Griffith's sprawling Babylon set from the movie Intolerance. Aside from shops, restaurants and a movie theater, it houses the Dolby Theatre, home of the Academy Awards. But from 1903 t0 1956, this spot was the site of Hotel Hollywood.

Over the years, Hotel Hollywood was considered *the* place to see and be seen. In 1919, it was the site of probably one of the stranger wedding nights in Hollywood history, when the hotel clerk refused to allow Rudolph Valentino to go up to his room with new bride Jean Acker until he could produce a marriage license. The night didn't get any better from there. Acker apparently locked Valentino out of the room, crying that she had made a terrible mistake.

In the late 1930s, Hearst syndicate gossip columnist Louella Parsons hosted a radio show from the hotel, featuring many of the day's biggest stars. Parson was the first, and arguably the most successful off the celebrity gossip columnists. Her byline appeared in all of Hearst's 700 newspapers. She was at the height of her power in those days, and was known to blacklist celebrities if they didn't give her a Christmas present. The source of Parson's power was a little unclear, unless you believe the rumors that surrounded a 1924 cruise on William Randolph Hearst's yacht, the Oneida.

According to the official story, producer-director William Ince missed the boat, literally and died of acute indigestion at his ranch. In reality, Ince died of a gunshot wound he sustained under mysterious circumstances on the Oneida. The rumor mill blamed Ince's death on Hearst himself, claiming that the media magnate mistook Ince for fellow guest Charlie Chaplin, who was rumored to be having an affair with Hearst mistress Marion Davies. Thinking he had caught the two in a stolen moment together, Hearst shot Ince in a jealous rage.

Parsons, who was still a relative unknown at the time, was a passenger on the boat. She had already endeared herself to Hearst by writing a favorable profile of Marion Davies. Following the cruise, she may have upped the ante and traded her silence for a nationwide syndication. However she managed it, Parsons launched gossip into the national mainstream. And she left a trail of ruined reputations in her wake.

Continue south on Highland Avenue, and turn right onto Hollywood Boulevard.

MABEL NORMAND'S WALK OF FAME STAR

6821 Hollywood Boulevard

Fatty Arbuckle was still in the midst of his second trial for the murder of Virginia Rappe when Hollywood was hit with a second celebrity murder. Director William Desmond Taylor was found dead in his home of two gunshot wounds to the heart. It was a scandal that nearly didn't happen. Paramount Studio executives were summoned to the scene before the police and spend the morning removing incriminating items and burning documents in the bungalow's fireplace, all-the-while stepping over Taylor's corpse. A Paramount-payroll doctor was even brought in, and he quickly ruled Taylor's death to be the result of a stomach hemorrhage. The police were unimpressed – they knew a bullet wound when they saw one.

Paramount executives had good reason to be nervous. At the time of his death, Taylor was at the center of fairly impressive love triangle. To start with, Taylor was involved with this young lady here, Mabel Normand, a silent film actress in Mack Sennett's studio who often appeared in Taylor's films. But that was just the tip of the iceberg.

Taylor was apparently also romancing twenty-two-year-old Paramount star Mary Miles Minter *and* Minter's overbearing stage mother, Charlotte Shelby. Worse, it turned out the Taylor wasn't really Taylor at all, but William Deanne-Tanner, who had abandoned his wife and daughter in New York in 1908 to pursue his film career. To top off the scandal, Taylor's butler, who went missing immediately after the murder, was revealed to be Taylor's own brother, who was on the run from the law at the time.

Both Normand and Minter were seen at Taylor's the night of his murder, as was a man in a heavy coat who was thought to be Charlotte Shelby in disguise. While both Normand and Minter were suspected of involvement in Taylor's murder, Charlotte Shelby was considered the most likely candidate, as she owned a gun of the same caliber as the murder weapon – a gun that conveniently went missing after the murder.

Still, no one was ever charged in the killing and Taylor's murder remains officially unsolved to this day. Normand and Minter were both ruined by the scandal and, although still young women, forced into early retirement.

Continue west on Hollywood Boulevard, stopping just short of the corner of Orange Drive.

LUPE VELEZ' WALK OF FAME STAR

6927 Hollywood Boulevard

Lupe Velez, also known as the Mexican Spitfire, was discovered by Douglas Fairbanks when she was still a teenager. She was known as much for her volatile love affairs as for her screen credits, including flings with John Gilbert, Gary Cooper and a marriage to Tarzan himself, Johnny Weissmuller. After her divorce from Weissmuller in 1938, Lupe's personal and professional life went downhill. In 1944, in debt and pregnant by a man who no longer wanted anything to do with her, Lupe decided to make her final exit in style.

She invited two close friends over for a final dinner. After they left, she donned a silver lame gown, penned a suicide note to Harald Ramond, the lover who had jilted her, swallowed a bottle of Seconal, lay down on her bed for a final slumber. Perhaps she should have choreographed the evening a little better. She apparently started vomiting and rushed into the bathroom, where she slipped and hit her head. She was found the next morning, drowned in her own toilet.

Retrace your steps just slightly to the courtyard in front of Grauman's Chinese Theatre.

GRAUMAN'S CHINESE THEATRE

6925 Hollywood Boulevard

And here we are at the final stop on our tour, Grauman's Chinese Theater, built in 1927. Although popular legend holds that Grauman stumbled on the idea of imbedding celebrities' hands and feet in cement when he, or even more romantically, actress Norma Talmadge, accidentally stepped in cement that had just been laid in front of the theater. In reality, it is unlikely that a calculating showman like Grauman owed his best publicity stunt to serendipity.

Earlier in the tour, I told you about Victor Kilian, whose ghost has been spotted here in the courtyard. The theatre itself is reported to have a pair of ghosts: an invisible stagehand who moves things and occasionally dims the lights in the employee locker room, and a ghostly little girl who attempts to pull down the stage curtains.

Now, if you've taken any ghost tour at all, you'll know that mischievous little girl gets around. In fact, she apparently runs across the street and haunts the lobby of the Roosevelt Hotel from time to time. And no respectable London Theatre would be without a phantom stagehand. But while these stories may not be the most convincing hauntings on our tour, it seems appropriate that we should finish with a tale of ghosts right out of Central Casting.

And that brings us to the end of our stroll through the strange, supernatural and scandalous side of Hollywood. I hope you've had fun and learned a little about the darker sides of the movie industries brightest lights. Enjoy the rest of your stay in Hollywood.

www.ingramcontent.com/pod-product-compliance
Lightning Source LLC
Chambersburg PA
CBHW060656030426

42337CB00017B/2647